Air Fryer Cookbook
Easy and Healthy, Low-Carb Air Fryer Recipes People Are Loving Delicious Meals That Will Convince You to Buy an Air Fryer

Brandon Hearn © 2019

Table of Contents

Introduction

If you're looking for an easy, modern way to cool healthy meals for your family, then the air fryer is the way to go. These recipes are low sodium and low carb, and you even get a calorie count to keep track of everything you're putting in your body. The air fryer will soon become one of the most useful appliances in your kitchen. In this book, you'll learn how to cook with the air fryer as well as many different, healthy recipes that you can try from morning to night. Just pick something that fits your mood, and don't be scared to be adventurous. From new meals to old family favorites, there's a recipe for everyone in this healthy cookbook.

Getting Started

Before we get started with delicious, mouth watering recipes, you need to understand what the air fryer is and how it works. The air fryer uses hot air in order to cook food so that you can use less oil. Most appliances rely on traditional cooking methods like conducting heat, but the air fryer goes against the trend. The air is the magic. It sucks in the air into the intake chamber and then cranks up the heat, raising the temperature of the air inside. The air is then passed through cooking cells where your meal is prepared. This can also be referred to as rapid air technology. The appliance cooks your meal and limits the amount of oil used by circulating that air around the food. The air keeps the heat instead of the oil!

Air Fryer Components

If you're new to the air fryer, then the parts may be a bit confusing at first glance. This section will help to clear up confusion so you can start using your air fryer straight away.

- **Cooking Chamber:** This is the part of your air fryer where your food will actually be placed to cook. The chamber will vary slightly from brand to brand. Some have normal cook baskets and some have walled cook baskets.

- **Heating Element:** This is the coil inside the fryer that will produce heat once electricity passes through it. The heating element will reach the desired temperature and then air is passed through the coil. The air heats up as it's passed through.

- **Fan & Grill:** This is what circulates the superheated air to cook your food.

- **Exhaust System:** This is where excess pressure is released so that no harmful buildup occurs. Most modern air fryers will also include a filter to get rid of dirt, which can keep unpleasant odors from building up in your air fryer.
- **Food Tray:** Depending on your air fryer, this may have boundary walls built within so that you can cook multiple dishes at once, and others have a handle that allow you to remove the tray with ease.

Some Common Features

Different air fryer brands will have different features, but there are some common air fryer features out there. Here are the basics, but be sure to read your manual to get to know your air fryer even better.

- **Assorted Cook Presets:** There are usually multiple pre-set cook settings, so you won't always have to worry about setting the right temperature. If you want to know the exact settings and parameters that your air fryer has, you'll find this information in your manual. These pre-settings can make using your air fryer so much easier.
- **Automated Temperature Control:** This will keep the temperature levels steady through the entire cooking session.
- **Touch Panel/Digital Screen:** This allows you to control your device without any hassle.
- **Buzzer:** This will let you know when the time is up so that you don't have to stand in the kitchen just to make sure that your food doesn't burn.

Some Benefits

There are many benefits to the air fryer. The biggest and most well known is that you reduce your oil intake by about eight percent, but here are a few more!

- They're easy to use and clean, so you don't have to worry about making a mess.
- You can improve your health and reach weight loss goals by cooking almost completely oil free meals.
- The air fryer will speed up your cooking time so you can provide healthy meals for your family without having to slave away in the kitchen.

Some Common Mistakes

Mistakes happen, but if you know the most common mistakes with the air fryer, then your adjustment period will take a little less time.

- **Not Giving it Room:** Your air fryer needs room to breath. Make sure that it isn't in cramped spaces or corners, or it simply won't work as well as it should.
- **Keeping it Plugged in:** The air fryer takes very little time to heat up, so you shouldn't keep it connected when it isn't in use.
- **Using Dark Trays & Dishes:** You don't want to use dark colored dishes or trays because dark material will absorb more heat. You'll be more likely to burn your food or experience uneven cooking.
- **Not Soaking Properly:** If you want help cleaning your air fryer, soak the compartments you need to clean in mild dish detergent and warm water so that cleaning is a breeze.

- **Scratching it During Cleaning:** You'll want to use simple sponges or clothes on the metal parts so that you don't scratch your air fryer up.

Steps to Use Your Air Fryer

Here are some basic steps to use your air fryer!

- **Step 1:** If you're using oil, lightly spray the food or basket with oil. This will keep food from sticking. However, rubbing it down is recommended since some cooking sprays can cause damage to your nit.
- **Step 2:** Even if you're using oil, you'll still need to pat dry excess liquid to keep your air fryer from smoking when cooking.
- **Step 3:** You'll have to shake your food gently after five minutes to cook evenly.
- **step 4:** This is the easiest step. You'll just need to follow directions according to your meal.
- **Step 5:** transfer your prepared food to the cook basket, following your recipe instructions. If you're baking a cake you'll need to pour your batter into a sperate dish before placing it on your cook tray.
- **Step 6:** You'll need to set your temperature and timer. Cook times are a guide, but it may not work best for every recipe.
- **Step 7:** You'll have to clean your oil catch frequently for the best air frying results.

Breakfast

Raspberry Rolls

Serves: 6
Time: 50 Minutes
Calories: 261
Protein: 6 Grams
Fat: 5 Grams
Carbs: 9 Grams
Ingredients:

- 1 Cup Whole Milk
- 4 Tablespoons Butter
- 2 Teaspoons Yeast
- ¼ Cup Sugar
- 1 Egg
- 3 ¼ Cup Flour

Filling:

- 8 Ounces Cream Cheese, Softened
- 12 Ounces Raspberries
- 1 Tablespoon Cornstarch

- 1 Lemon, Zested & Grated
- 5 Tablespoons Sugar
- 1 Teaspoon Vanilla Extract, Pure

Directions:

1. Get out a bowl and mix your yeast, flour and sugar together until well combined.
2. Add in your egg and milk, stirring until a dough forms. Allow it to rise for thirty minutes before transferring it to a work surface. Roll well.
3. Get out a bowl and mix your sugar, cream cheese, lemon zest and vanilla together. Stir well and spread this mixture over the dough.
4. In another bowl mix your cornstarch and raspberries, spreading it over your cream cheese mixture.
5. Roll your dough, cutting it into medium pieces. Place them in the air fryer, cooking at 350 for a half hour.
6. Serve warm or room temperature.

Vegetable Frittata

Serves: 4
Time: 25 Minutes
Calories: 77
Protein: 8 Grams
Fat: 3 Grams
Carbs: 5 Grams
Ingredients:

- ½ Cup Red Bell Pepper, Chopped

- 1/3 Cup Carrot, Grated

- 1/3 Cup Onion, Minced

- 1 Teaspoon Olive Oil

- 6 Egg Whites

- 1 Egg

- 1/3 Cup Milk, Two Percent

- 1 Tablespoon Parmesan Cheese, Grated

Directions:

1. Start by getting out a six by two inch pan, throwing in your red bell pepper, carrot, olive oil and onion. Place your pan in the air fryer, allowing it to cook

for four to six minutes. Shake your basket once during this time. Your vegetable should be tender.

2. Get out a medium bowl while you're cooking your vegetables, and beat your egg whites, egg, and milk together until it's mixed well.

3. Pour this egg mixture over your vegetables, and then sprinkle the top with parmesan cheese. Place the pan back in the air fryer, and cook for another four to six minutes. Your frittata should be puffy but set well.

4. Serve warm.

Salmon Frittata

Serves: 4
Time: 30 Minutes
Calories: 97
Protein: 11 Grams
Carbs: 3 Grams
Carbs: 7 Grams
Ingredients:

- ½ Teaspoon Thyme, Dried

- 4 Eggs Whites

- 1 Egg

- Olive Oil as Needed for Greasing

- ½ Cup Brown Rice, Cooked

- ½ Cup Salmon, Cooked & Flaked

- ½ Cup Baby Spinach, Fresh

- ¼ Cup Red Bell Pepper, Chopped

- 1 Tablespoon Parmesan, Grated

Directions:

1. Get out a six by two inch pan, rubbing it down with olive oil before setting it to the side.

2. Get outa small bowl and beat your egg whites, egg, and thyme together until it is mixed well.

3. Take your prepared pan and stir together your brown rice, spinach, red bell pepper and salmon pour in the egg mixture over your rice, and then top with parmesan.

4. Bake for fifteen minutes. The frittata should be set, puffed and golden brown. Serve warm.

Carrot & Cinnamon Muffins

Serves: 8
Time: 35 Minutes
Calories: 201
Protein: 4 Grams
Fat: 7 Grams
Carbs: 32 Grams
Ingredients:

- 1 ½ Cups Pastry Flour, Whole Wheat
- 1 Teaspoon Baking Powder, Low Sodium
- 1/3 Cup Brown Sugar
- 1 Egg
- 2 Egg Whites
- ½ Teaspoon Ground Cinnamon
- 2/3 Cup Almond Milk
- 3 Tablespoons Safflower Oil
- ½ Cup carrots, Shredded Fine
- 1/3 Cup Golden Raisins, Chopped

Directions:

1. Get out a bowl and combine your baking powder, brown sugar, cinnamon, and flour. Mix well, and then get out a small bowl.

2. In your small bowl combine your egg whites, egg, almond milk and oil. Mix well, and sir until the dry ingredients are combined. Make sure that you don't overbeat your batter. It is okay to have some lumps in the batter still.

3. Stir in your raisins and shredded carrots gently. Once again you need to make sure you don't overmix your batter. Get out sixteen foil muffin cups, doubling hem to make eight cups. Put four of them into your air fryer, filling them ¾ full with batter. Bake for twelve to seventeen minutes. Repeat with the remaining batter, and allow them to cool for ten minutes before serving.

Breakfast Bread Pudding

Serves: 4
Time: 35 Minutes
Calories: 261
Protein: 5 Grams
Fat: 7 Grams
Carbs: 8 Grams
Ingredients:

- ½ Cup Apple, Peeled, Cored & Roughly Chopped

- 2 Teaspoons Cornstarch

- ¾ Cup Whole Milk

- ¾ Cup Water

- ½ lb. White Bread, Cubed

- 5 Tablespoons Honey, Raw

- 1 Teaspoon Vanilla Extract, Pure

- 2 Teaspoons Cinnamon, Ground

- 1 1/3 Cup Flour

- 3 Ounces Butter, Softened

- 3/5 Cup Brown Sugar

Directions:

1. Mix your apple milk, bread, water, honey, cinnamon, cornstarch and vanilla. Whisk well, and then get out a separate bowl. Mix your flour, sugar and butter. Stir until you get a crumbly mixture.

2. Press half of your crumble into the bottom f your air fryer and then add the bread and apple mix. Top with the remaining crumble, and cook at 350 for twenty-two minutes.

3. Serve warm or room temperature.

Berry Pancake

Serves: 4
Time: 26 Minutes
Calories: 154
Protein: 7 Grams
Fat: 5 Grams
Carbs: 21 Grams
Ingredients:

- 2 Egg Whites / 1 Egg
- ½ Cup Pastry Flour, Whole Wheat
- ½ Cup Milk, Two Percent
- 1 Teaspoon Vanilla Extract, Pure
- 1 Tablespoon Butter, Unsalted & Melted
- ½ Cup Blueberries, Fresh
- ½ Cup Raspberries, Fresh / 1 Cup Strawberries, Fresh & Sliced

Directions:

1. Get out a medium bowl and get out a hand mixer. Beat your egg whites, pasty flour, egg, vanilla and milk until thoroughly combined. Get out a pastry brush and a six by two inch pan.

2. Brush down your pan with melted butter, and then immediately pour your batter into the pan and place the basket back in the fryer. Bake for twelve to sixteen minutes. Your pancake should be golden brown and puffed.

3. Remove from the pan, and then when the top falls add your berries. Serve immediately so it's still fresh.

Lunch

Pork Burger

Serves: 2
Time: 35 Minutes
Calories: 470
Protein: 22 Grams
Fat: 42 Grams
Carbs: 1 Gram
Ingredients:

- ½ lb Pork, Minced
- 1 Tablespoon Tomato Puree
- 1 Tablespoon Mixed Herbs
- 2 Teaspoon Garlic Powder
- 2 Bread Buns, Halved
- 1 Teaspoon Mustard
- 1 Onion, Chopped
- 1 Teaspoon Basil
- 1/8 Teaspoon Sea Salt, Fine

- 1/8 Teaspoon Black Pepper

Assembling:

- 1 Onion, Sliced into 2 Inch Rings
- 2 Lettuce Leaves
- 4 Slices Cheddar Cheese
- 1 Tomato, Sliced into 2 Inch Rings

Directions:

1. Start by getting out a bowl and mixing your main ingredients together using your hands. Form two patties from the mixture before preheating your air fryer to 370. Put your pork patties inside, and cook for fifteen minutes.

2. Slide the fryer basket out, turning your patties, and then reduce the temperature to 350. Cook for an additional five minutes. Assemble your burgers before serving.

Blue Cheese & Beet Salad

Serves: 6
Time: 25 Minutes
Calories: 100
Protein: 5 Grams
Fat: 4 Grams
Carbs: 10 Grams
Ingredients:

- 6 Beets, Peeled & Quartered
- ¼ Cup Blue Cheese, Crumbled
- 1 Tablespoon Olive Oil
- 1/8 Teaspoon Sea Salt, Fine
- 1/8 Teaspoon Black Pepper

Directions:

1. Start by placing your beets in the air fryer, cooking at 350 for fourteen minutes. Transfer them to a bowl, and then add your remaining ingredients.
2. Toss well, and then serve immediately.

Zucchini Casserole

Serves: 8
Time: 30 Minutes
Calories: 133
Protein: 5 Grams
Fat: 3 Grams
Carbs: 10 Grams
Ingredients:

- 1 Cup Vegetable Stock

- 2 Tablespoons Olive Oil

- 2 Sweet Potatoes, Peeled & Cut into Wedges

- 8 Zucchini, Cut into Wedges

- 2 Yellow Onions, Chopped

- 1 Cup Coconut Milk

- 1 Tablespoon Soy Sauce, Low Sodium

- ¼ Teaspoon Thyme

- 1/8 Teaspoon Sea Salt, Fine

- 1/8 Teaspoon Black Pepper

- ¼ Teaspoon Rosemary

- 4 Tablespoons Dill, Fresh & Chopped

- ½ Teaspoon Basil, Fresh & Chopped

Directions:

1. Heat up a pan that fits in your air fryer over medium heat with oil. Add in your onions and cook for two minutes. You'll need to stir to make sure that it doesn't burn. Add in your thyme, rosemary, zucchini, potato, salt, pepper, stock, basil, milk, dill and soy sauce. Stir well, and then place it in your air fryer.
2. Cook at 360 for fourteen minutes, and serve warm.

Greek Veggie Skillet

Serves: 4
Time: 30 Minutes
Calories: 97
Protein: 15 Grams
Fat: 1 Gram
Carbs: 5 Grams
Ingredients:

- 1/2 lb. Lean Ground Beef, 96 Percent

- 1 Onion, Chopped

- 2 Cloves Garlic, Minced

- 2 Tomatoes, Chopped

- 2 Tablespoons Feta Cheese, Crumbled & Low Sodium

- 1/3 Cup Beef Broth, Low Sodium

- 2 Tablespoons Lemon Juice, Squeezed Fresh

- 2 Cups Baby Spinach

Directions:

1. Start by getting out a six by two inch pan, and crumble your beef. Cook for three to seven minutes, making sure your meat browns using the air fryer. You'll need to stir once during the cooking time. Drain away any liquid or excess fat.

2. Add in your garlic, onion and tomatoes, cooking for four to eight more minutes. Your onion should become tender, and then add in your lemon juice, beef broth and spinach. Cook for another additional two to four minutes. Your spinach should be wilted.

3. Sprinkle with feta cheese before serving.

Winter Vegetable Medley

Serves: 2 / **Time:** 30 Minutes
Calories: 50
Protein: 2 Grams
Fat: 3 Grams / **Carbs:** 5 Grams
Ingredients:

- 1 Parsnip, Small, Peeled & Sliced into 2 Inch Thickness

- 1 Tablespoon Thyme, Fresh & Chopped

- 1 Cup Butternut Squash, Chopped

- 1 Cup Celery, Chopped

- 2 Red Onions, Small & Sliced into Wedges

- 2 Teaspoons Olive Oil

- 1/8 Teaspoon Sea Salt, Fine

- 1/8 Teaspoon Black Pepper

Directions:

1. Start by heating your air fryer to 200, and then get outa bowl. Mix together your celery, butternut, squash, parsnips, thyme and red onion. Season with olive oil, salt, and pepper.

2. Pour your mixture into the air fryer basket, and then allow it to cook for sixteen minutes before serving.

Steak & Vegetables

Serves: 4
Time: 30 Minutes
Calories: 194
Protein: 31 Grams
Fat: 6 Grams
 Carbs: 7 Grams
Ingredients:

- 2 Tablespoon Balsamic Vinegar

- 2 Teaspoons Olive oil

- ½ Teaspoon Marjoram

- 1/8 Teaspoon Black Pepper

- ¾ lb. Round Steak, Sliced into 1 Inch Pieces

- 16 Button Mushrooms

- 1 Cup Cherry Tomatoes

- 1 Red Bell Pepper, Sliced

Directions:

1. Start by getting out a bowl and mix together your marjoram, black pepper, balsamic vinegar and olive oil. Add your steak in, stirring to coat well. Allow it to marinate for ten minutes.

2. Make your kebabs on eight bamboo skewers, alternating ingredients before putting your kebabs in the air fryer.

3. Grill for five to seven minutes. Your beef should be browned. Serve warm.

Barbecue Chicken

Serves: 4
Time: 30 Minutes
Calories: 182
Protein: 33 Grams
Fat: 2 Grams
Carbs: 7 Grams
Ingredients:

- 1/3 Cup Tomato Sauce, No Salt Added
- 2 Tablespoons Grainy Mustard, Low Sodium
- 2 Tablespoons Apple Cider Vinegar
- 1 Jalapeno Pepper, Minced
- 2 Cloves Garlic, Minced
- 3 Tablespoons Onion, Minced
- 4 Chicken Breasts, Boneless, Skinless & Low Sodium

Directions:

1. Start by mixing together your onion, tomato sauce, apple cider vinegar, mustard, honey, onion, garlic and jalapeno.
2. Brush your chicken with the sauce and then grill for ten minutes.

3. Take it out of your air fryer basket to turn it and coat with more sauce. Grill for another five minutes. Turn once more, brushing it down with sauce and cooking for another three to five minutes.

4. Serve warm.

Chicken & Spinach Salad

Serves: 4
Time: 30 Minutes
Calories: 214
Protein: 28 Grams
Fat: 7 Grams
Carbs: 7 Grams
Ingredients:

- 3 Chicken Breasts, Boneless & Skinless, Low Sodium & Chopped into 1 Inch Cubes
- 5 Teaspoon Olive Oil
- ½ Teaspoon Thyme, Dried
- 1 Red Onion, Sliced
- 1 Red Bell Pepper, Sliced
- 1 Zucchini, Small & Cut into Strips
- 3 Tablespoons Lemon Juice, Fresh
- 6 Cups Baby Spinach, Fresh

Directions:

1. Get out a large bowl and mix your chicken with your thyme and olive oil. Toss until it's coated and then get out a medium metal bowl. Roast your chicken for eight minutes in this bowl in the air fryer.

2. Add in your red bell pepper, red onion and zucchini, roasting for another eight to twelve minutes. You'll need to stir once during this time.

3. Remove the bowl from the air fryer, and then add in your lemon juice. Stir, and then place your spinach in the serving bowl. Toss to combine, and serve warm.

Ratatouille

Serves: 4
Time: 30 Minutes
Calories: 69
Protein: 2 Grams
Fat: 2 Grams
Carbs: 11 Grams
Ingredients:

- 4 Roma Tomatoes, Seeded & Chopped
- 3 Cloves Garlic, Sliced
- 1 Red Bell Pepper, Chopped
- 1 Yellow Bell Pepper, Chopped
- 1 Baby eggplant, Peeled & Chopped
- 1 Small Onion, Chopped
- 1 Teaspoon Olive Oil
- 1 Teaspoon Italian Seasoning

Directions:

1. Get out a medium bowl and combine your egg plant, bell peppers, garlic, onion, and tomatoes. Season with Italian seasoning and olive oil.

2. Put your bowl in your air fryer, roasting for twelve to sixteen minutes. Stir once during this time, and serve warm.

Snacks

Spiced Banana Chips

Serves: 4
Time: 25 Minutes
Calories: 121
Protein: 3 Grams
Fat: 1 Grams
Carbs: 3 Grams
Ingredients:

- 4 Bananas, Peeled & Sliced
- 1/8 Teaspoon Sea Salt, Fine
- 1 Teaspoon Olive Oil
- ½ Teaspoon Turmeric Powder
- ½ Teaspoon Chaat Masala

Directions:

1. Get out a bowl and mix all of your ingredients together, letting them sit for ten minutes.
2. Heat your air fryer to 360, and then cook for fifteen minutes. Flip once during this time and serve once cooled down.

Spicy Chicken Meatballs

Serves: 4
Time: 25 Minutes
Calories: 185
Protein: 29 Grams
Fat: 7 Grams
Carbs: 5 Grams
Ingredients:

- 1 Red Onion, Minced
- 2 Cloves Garlic, Minced
- 1 Jalapeno Pepper, Minced
- 2 Teaspoons Olive Oil
- 3 Tablespoons Almonds, Ground
- 1 Egg / 1 lb. Ground Chicken
- 1 Teaspoon Thyme

Directions:

1. Get a six by two inch pan out and combine your garlic, jalapeno, olive oil and red onion. Bake for three to four minutes. Your vegetables should be tender and crisp before you transfer them to a bowl.

2. Mix in your egg, almonds, and thyme to your vegetables before adding in your chicken. Mix until well combined, and then form twenty-four meatballs.

3. Bake for eight to ten minutes before serving.

Fruit & Chicken Bruschetta

Serves: 4
Time: 25 Minutes
Calories: 175
Protein: 9 Grams
Fat: 4 Grams
Carbs: 30 Grams
Ingredients:

- 1 Tablespoon Butter, Unsalted & Room Temperature
- 3 Slices Whole Wheat Bread, Low Sodium
- ½ Cup Peaches, Peeled & Chopped
- ½ Cup Strawberries, Fresh & Chopped
- ½ Cup Blueberries, Fresh
- ¼ Cup Canned Chicken Breasts, Low Sodium & Drained
- 1 Tablespoon Lemon Juice, Fresh
- 1 Tablespoon Honey, Raw

Directions:

1. Start by spreading your butter on the bread, and then place it in your air fryer. Bake for three to five minutes. It should turn a light golden brown.

2. Get out a small bowl and mix your blueberries, chicken, strawberries, peaches and lemon juice together.

3. Take the bread out of your air fryer, and top each slice with the mixture before drizzling honey over it. Place it back into your air fryer. Make sure that you don't overcrowd it, so do it in batches if you have to.

4. Bake for two to five minutes. Your fruit should start to caramelize, and then cut each slice into quarters before serving warm.

Spiced Sweet Potato Fries

Serves: 4
Time: 30 Minutes
Calories: 125
Protein: 7 Grams
Fat: 4 Grams
Carbs: 17 Grams
Ingredients:

- 2 Sweet potatoes, Large & Cut into Sticks

- 1 Teaspoon Ground Paprika

- 1 Teaspoon Ground Cumin

- ½ Teaspoon Garlic Powder

- ½ Teaspoon Cayenne Pepper

- 1/8 Teaspoon Black Pepper

- 1 Cup Greek, Low Fat Yogurt

- 2 Teaspoons Olive Oil

Directions:

1. Get out a bowl of cold water and soak your cut sweet potato in them while you prepare your dip.

2. Get out a small bowl and mix your paprika, garlic, cumin, cayenne and black pepper.

3. Get out a small bowl, whisking half of your spice mixture into your yogurt, and refrigerate the dish.

4. drain your sweet potatoes, patting them dry, and then put them in a large bowl. Sprinkle with olive oil before tossing. Make sure that they're coated thoroughly.

5. Sprinkle the remaining seasoning over your fries after you take them from the water, and then place them in the air fryer basket. Cook for eight to twelve minutes. They should be golden brown and crisp.

6. Serve warm with your dip.

Pear Cinnamon Chips

Serves: 4
Time: 30 Minutes
Calories: 30
Protein: 7 Grams
Fat: 0 Grams
Carbs: 8 Grams
Ingredients:

- 2 Pears, Firm & Cut into 1/8 Inch Thick Slices

- 1 Tablespoon Lemon Juice, Fresh

- ½ Teaspoon Cinnamon, Ground

- 1/8 Teaspoon Cardamom, Ground

Directions:

1. Start by chopping your pear. You will need to remove the core from the larger slices, and sprinkle all of your slices with cardamom, cinnamon and lemon juice.

2. Place your smaller chips in your air fryer basket, and air fry for three to five minutes. You'll need to shake the basket once, and they should be a golden brown.

3. Do another batch with your larger slices, which will take six to eight minutes. Once again, you'll need to shake at least once during this time, and they should be golden brown.

4. Remove your chips from your air fryer, and allow them to cool before serving. They will last up to two days in an airtight container when stored at room temperature.

Roasted Grape Dip

Serves: 6
Time: 25 Minutes
Calories: 71
Protein: 4 Grams
Fat: 0 Grams
Carbs: 15 Grams
Ingredients:

- 2 Cups Red Grapes, Seedless, Rinsed & Patted Dry
- 1 Tablespoon Apple Cider Vinegar
- 1 Tablespoon Honey, Raw
- 1 Cup Greek Yogurt, Low Fat
- 2 Tablespoons Milk, Two Percent
- 2 Tablespoons Basil, Minced & Fresh

Directions:

1. Start by sprinkling your grapes with honey and apple cider vinegar. Make sure they're well coated, and roast your grapes for eight to twelve minutes. They should be shriveled but soft still. Take them out of your air fryer.

2. Get out a bowl and mix together your yogurt and milk.

3. Blend your grapes and basil, and mix everything together.

4. Chill for about two hours before serving.

Chicken Meatballs

Serves: 4
Time: 30 Minutes
Calories: 98
Protein: 14 Grams
Fat: 3 Grams
Carbs: 4 Grams
Ingredients:

- 2 Teaspoons Olive Oil

- ¼ Cup Red Bell Pepper, Minced

- ¼ Cup Onion, Minced

- 2 Vanilla Wafers, Crushed

- ½ Teaspoon Thyme

- ½ lb. Ground Chicken

- 1 Egg White

Directions:

1. Star by getting out aa six by two inch pan, and mix together your onion, olive oil and red bell pepper. Place it in the air fryer, and cook for three to five minutes. The vegetables should still be tender.

2. Get out a bowl and mix together your crushed wafers, cooked vegetables, thyme and egg white. Make sure that it's well combined.

3. Add in your chicken, and gently combine the mixture together. Make sure not to overmix or your meatballs could fall apart.

4. Form sixteen meatballs from this mixture, and place them in your air fryer. Cook for ten to fifteen minutes.

Sweet Potato Chips

Serves: 4
Time: 15 Minutes
Calories: 238
Protein: 1.9 Grams
Fat: 10.7 Grams
Carbs: 35.1 Grams
Ingredients:

- 500 Grams Sweet Potatoes

- 3 Tablespoons Olive Oil

- 1/8 Teaspoon Chili Powder

- ¼ Teaspoon Cinnamon

- 1/8 Teaspoon Sea Salt, Fine

- 1/8 Teaspoon Black Pepper

Directions:

1. Start by heating up your air fryer to 350, and then slice your sweet potato to make thin chips. It's easiest if you have a mandolin to use.

2. Drizzle your potato chips with olive oil before sprinkling your slat, pepper and cinnamon on top. Make sure it's well coated, so toss as necessary.

3. Put your chips in the basket, cooking for ten minutes. You'll need to shake once midway through to keep them from sticking. Once golden brown and crisp transfer to a bowl and serve immediately or cooled down.

Dinner

Crispy Lamb

Serves: 4
Time: 40 Minutes
Calories: 230
Protein: 12 Grams
Fat: 2 Grams
Carbs: 10 Grams
Ingredients:

- 1 Tablespoon Bread Crumbs
- 2 Tablespoons Macadamia Nuts, Toasted & Crushed
- 1 Tablespoons Olive Oil
- 1 Clove Garlic, Minced
- 28 Ounces Rack of Lamb
- 1/8 Teaspoon Sea Salt, Fine
- 1/8 Teaspoon Black Pepper

- 1 Egg
- 1 Tablespoon Rosemary, Chopped

Directions:

1. Start by getting out a bowl and mix your garlic and oil. Stir until well combined, and then season your lamb with salt and pepper. Brush down your lamb with your garlic and oil mixture.

2. Get out a different bowl and mix your breadcrumbs, rosemary and mixed nuts.

3. Put your eggs in a different bowl, and whisk them.

4. Dip your lamb into the egg mixture, then the macadamia mix, and then place it in the air fryer basket. Cook at 360 for twenty-five minutes. Increase your heat to 400, and cook for an additional 5 minutes. Serve warm.

Spicy Steak

Serves: 4
Time: 20 Minutes
Calories: 160
Protein: 24 Grams
Fat: 6 Grams
Carbs: 1 Gram
Ingredients:

- 1 Teaspoon Ground Cumin

- 2 Tablespoons Salsa, Low Sodium

- 1 Tablespoon Chipotle Pepper, Minced

- 1 Tablespoon Apple Cider Vinegar

- 1/8 Teaspoon Red Pepper Flakes

- 1/8 Teaspoon Black Pepper

- ¾ lb. Sirloin Tip Steak, Cut into 4 Pieces, Pounded to 1/3 Inch Thick

Directions:

1. Get out a small bowl and mix your chipotle pepper, apple cider vinegar, salsa, cumin, red pepper flakes and black pepper together. Rub the mixture

into your steak pieces, letting it stand for fifteen minutes so the flavors marinate.

2. Grill your steaks using the air fryer for six to nine minutes. You'll need to do them in batches. When ready to serve slice your steaks thinly against the grain.

Healthy Fried Chicken

Serves: 4
Time: 30 Minutes
Calories: 217
Protein: 34 Grams
Fat: 6 Grams
Carbs: 6 Grams
Ingredients:

- 4 Chicken Breasts, Boneless, Skinless, Low Sodium & Pounded to ½ Inch Thickness
- ½ Cup Buttermilk
- 2 Tablespoons Cornstarch
- 1 Teaspoon Thyme
- ½ Cup All Purpose Flour
- 1 Egg White
- 1 Teaspoon Paprika
- 1 Tablespoon Olive Oil

Directions:

1. Start by getting out a shallow bowl and mix your buttermilk and chicken together. Allow it to stand for ten minutes, and then get out another shallow bowl.

2. In the new bowl mix your cornstarch, thyme, flour and paprika.

3. In a different small bowl whisk your olive oil and egg white together. Stir the egg mixture into the flour one, and make sure it mixes together until evenly moistened.

4. Remove your chicken from your buttermilk, shaking off any excess liquid, and then dip it into your flour mixture.

5. Place your chicken in the air fryer for seventeen to twenty-three minutes. Serve warm.

Pork Satay

Serves: 4
Time: 30 Minutes
Calories: 194
Protein: 25 Grams
Fat: 7 Grams
Carbs: 7 Grams
Ingredients:

- 1 lb. Pork Tenderloin, Cut into 1 ½ Inch Cubes
- ¼ Cup Onion, Minced
- 2 Cloves Garlic, Minced
- 1 Jalapeno Pepper, Minced
- 2 Tablespoons Lime Juice, Fresh
- 2 Tablespoons Coconut Milk
- 2 Teaspoon Curry Powder
- 2 tablespoons Peanut Butter, Unsalted

Directions:

1. Start by getting out a bowl and mixing your garlic, onion, pork, lime juice, coconut milk, jalapeno, curry powder and peanut butter until it's well combined. Allow it to marinate for ten minutes at room temperature.

2. Use a slotted spoon to remove the pork from the marinade, and reserve the marinade for later.

3. Get out eight bamboo skewers, and thread your pork onto them. Grill in your air fryer for nine to fourteen minutes, brushing them down once with the marinade. Serve warm.

Espresso Tenderloin

Serves: 4
Time: 30 Minutes
Calories: 177
Protein: 23 Grams
Fat: 5 Grams
Carbs: 10 Grams
Ingredients:

- 1 Tablespoon Brown Sugar, Packed
- 2 Teaspoons Espresso Powder
- 1 Teaspoon Paprika
- ½ teaspoon Marjoram
- 1 Tablespoon Honey, Raw
- 1 Tablespoon Lemon Juice, Fresh
- 2 Teaspoons Olive Oil
- 1 lb. Pork Tenderloin

Directions:

1. Get out a small bowl and mix together your marjoram, espresso powder, brown sugar and paprika. Stir in your olive oil, lemon juice and honey. Make sure it's mixed well.

2. Spread this mixture over your pork tenderloin, letting your meat marinate for ten minutes at room temperature.

3. Roast in your air fryer basket for nine to eleven minutes. Slice meat and serve warm.

Greek Kebabs

Serves: 4
Time: 30 Minutes
Calories: 163
Protein: 27 Grams
Fat: 4 Grams
Carbs: 4 Grams
Ingredients:

- 3 Tablespoons Lemon Juice Fresh
- 2 Teaspoons Olive Oil
- 2 Tablespoons Flat Leaf Parsley, Fresh & Chopped
- ½ Teaspoon Oregano
- ½ Teaspoon Mint, Dried
- 1 lb. Chicken Breast, Boneless, Skinless & Low Sodium
- 1 Cup Cherry Tomatoes
- 1 Yellow Summer Squash, Small & Chopped into 1 Inch Cube

Directions:

1. Start by mixing your olive oil, lemon juice, mint, parsley and oregano together before adding in your chicken. Stir until it's well coated, and allow it to stand at room temperature for ten minutes to marinate.

2. Thread your thicken, tomatoes and squash on eight bamboo skewers by alternating the items.

3. Brush your kebabs down with the marinade, and then grill for fifteen minutes. Serve warm.

Tandoori Chicken

Serves: 4
Time: 30 Minutes
Calories: 197
Protein: 33 Grams
Fat: 5 Grams
Carbs: 4 Grams
Ingredients:

- 2/3 Cup Yogurt, Plain & Low Fat

- 2 Tablespoons Lemon Juice, Fresh

- 2 Teaspoon Curry Powder

- ½ Teaspoon Ground Cinnamon

- 2 Teaspoons Olive Oil

- 2 Cloves Garlic, Minced

- 4 Chicken Breasts, 5 Ounces Each, Boneless, Skinless & Low Sodium

Directions:

1. Start by whisking together your lemon juice, curry powder, cinnamon, yogurt, garlic and olive oil together using a medium bowl.

2. Get out a sharp knife and cut thin slashes into your chicken, and then coat it with the yogurt mixture. Allow it to marinate for ten minutes at room temperature, but you can marinate it up to twenty-four hours.

3. Shake off any excess liquid from the chicken, and discard the remaining marinade. Roast your chicken for ten minutes, and then roast for eight to thirteen minutes. Serve warm.

Mexican Chicken Stir Fry

Serves: 4
Time: 30 Minutes
Calories: 211
Protein: 29 Grams
Fat: 4 Grams
Carbs: 13 Grams
Ingredients:

- 1 lb. Chicken Breast, Boneless, Skinless, Low Sodium & Cut into 1 Inch Cubes
- 1 Red Bell Pepper, Chopped
- 1 Onion, Chopped
- 2 Teaspoons Olive Oil
- 1 Jalapeno Pepper, Minced
- 2/3 Cup Black Beans, Canned, Low Sodium, Rinsed & Drained
- ½ Cup Salsa, Low Sodium
- 2 Teaspoons Chili Powder

Directions:

1. Start by mixing your onion, chicken, jalapeno, olive oil and bell pepper together. Stir fry in your air fryer for ten minutes. You'll need to stir once during this cooking time.

2. Add in your chili powder, black beans and salsa, cooking for another seven to ten minutes. You'll need to stir once during this time. Serve warm.

Salmon & Carrot

Serves: 2
Time: 30 Minutes
Calories: 253
Protein: 31 Grams
Fat: 9 Grams
Carbs: 12 Grams
Ingredients:

- 1 Fennel Bulb, Sliced Thin

- 1 Carrot, Large, Peeled & Sliced

- 2 Salmon Fillet, 5 Ounces Each

- ¼ Cup Sour Cream, Low Fat

- ¼ Teaspoon Black Pepper, Ground Coarse

- 1 Onion, Small & Sliced Thin

Directions:

1. Start by combining your onion, fennel and carrot in a bowl, tossing it until it's well mixed. Get out a six inch metal pan, pouring your vegetable mixture

into it, and turn your air fryer to roast. Roast for four minutes. Your vegetables should be tender and crisp.

2. Remove your pan from the air fryer, and then stir in your sour cream before sprinkling the mixture with pepper. Top with your salmon fillets.

3. Place your pan back in the air fryer, roasting for another nine to ten minutes. The salmon should flake with a fork.

Scallops with Vegetables

Serves: 4 / **Time:** 25 Minutes
Calories: 124 / **Protein:** 14 Grams
Fat: 3 Grams / **Carbs:** 11 Grams
Ingredients:

- 1 Cup Green Beans

- 1 Cup Frozen Peas

- 1 Cup Broccoli, Frozen & Chopped

- 2 Teaspoons Olive Oil

- ½ Teaspoon Basil

- ½ Teaspoon Oregano / 12 Ounces Sea Scallops

Directions:

1. Get out a large bowl and toss together your broccoli, peas and green beans along with your olive oil. Place this mixture into your air fryer basket, frying for four to six minutes. they vegetables should be tender and crisp.

2. take your vegetables out of the air fryer basket, sprinkling with your seasoning before setting them to the side.

3. Next, place your scallops in the basket, cooking for four to five minutes. The scallops should be firm. They need to reach an internal temperature of 145

to be safe to eat. Toss your scallops with your vegetables before serving warm.

Snapper & Fruit

Serves: 4

Time: 30 Minutes

Calories: 245

Protein: 25 Grams

Fat: 4 Grams

Carbs: 28 Grams

Ingredients:

- 4 Red Snapper Fillets, 4 Ounces Each
- 3 Nectarines, Halved & Pitted
- 2 Teaspoon Olive Oil
- 3 Plums, Halved & Pitted
- 1 Cup Red Grapes
- 1 Tablespoon Honey, Raw
- ½ Teaspoon Thyme
- 1 Tablespoon Lemon Juice, Fresh

Directions:

1. Put your snapper in the air fryer basket before drizzling it with olive oil. Fry for four minutes.
2. Remove your fish from the basket, and then add in your plums, grapes and nectarines. Drizzle with honey and lemon juice. Sprinkle your thyme over top, and return it to the basket. Cook for five to nine more minutes. Your fish should become flaky.
3. Serve warm.

Tuna & Fruit Kebabs

Serves: 4 / **Time:** 30 Minutes
Calories: 181 / **Protein:** 18 Grams
Fat: 0 Grams / **Carbs:** 13 Grams
Ingredients:

- 1 b Tune Steaks, Cut into 1 Inch Cubes
- ½ Cup Pineapplc Chunks, Caned, Drained & Juice Reserved
- ½ Cup Red Grapes, Large
- 1 Tablespoon Honey, Raw
- 2 Teaspoon Ginger, Fresh & Grated
- 1 Teaspoon Olive Oil
- Pinch Cayenne Pepper

Directions:

1. Thread your pineapple, grapes and tuna through eight bamboo skewers that will fit in your air fryer.

2. Get out a small bowl and whisk a tablespoon of your pineapple juice, honey, ginger, cayenne and olive oil together. Brush your kebabs down with this mixture, and allow them to marinate for ten minutes.

3. Grill your kebabs for eight to twelve minutes. Your tuna should reach an internal temperature of at least 145 before it's considered safe to eat.

4. Rush with remaining sauce before serving warm.

Tofu with Broccoli

Serves: 4
Time: 20 Minutes
Calories: 91
Protein: 2.9 Grams
Fat: 8 Grams
Carbs: 3.7 Grams
Ingredients:

- ½ Block Firm Tofu, Squared
- 2 Cups Broccoli Florets
- 1/8 Teaspoon Sea Salt, Fine
- 1/8 Teaspoon Black Pepper
- 2 Tablespoons Olive Oil
- 1 Teaspoon Chili Peppers

Directions:

1. Start by heating your air fryer to 375, and then get outa baking dish.

2. In your baking dish combine your tofu squares, olive oil, salt, pepper and broccoli florets. Make sure it's all mixed well.

3. Cook for five to ten minutes. Your tofu should turn a nice golden brown, and then serve warm and topped with chili pepper.

Side Dishes

Roasted Pumpkin

Serves: 4
Time: 25 Minutes
Calories: 200
Protein: 4 Grams
Fat: 5 Grams
Carbs: 7 Grams
Ingredients:

- 1 ½ lbs. Pumpkin Deseeded & Chopped Roughly

- 3 Cloves Garlic, Minced

- 1 Tablespoon Olive Oil

- 1/8 Teaspoon Brown Sugar

- 1/8 Teaspoon Nutmeg, Ground

- 1/8 Teaspoon Cinnamon, Ground

- 1/8 Teaspoon Sea Salt, Fine

Directions:

1. Place all of your ingredients in your air fryer basket, making sure that your pumpkin is coated well.

2. Cook at 370 for twelve minutes, and serve immediately.

Herb Tomatoes

Serves: 4
Time: 25 Minutes
Calories: 112
Protein: 4 Grams
Fat: 1 Gram
Carbs: 4 Grams
Ingredients:

- 4 Tomatoes, Big, Halved & Insides Removed
- 1/8 Teaspoon Sea Salt, Fine
- 1/8 Teaspoon Black Pepper
- 1 Tablespoon Olive Oil
- 2 Cloves Garlic, Minced
- ½ Teaspoon Thyme, Fresh & Chopped

Directions:

1. Mix your tomatoes with salt, pepper, garlic, thyme and oil. Toss well, and heat your air fryer to 390.
2. Cook for fifteen minutes, and serve warm.

Roasted Parsnips

Serves: 6
Time: 50 Minutes
Calories: 124
Protein: 4 Grams
Fat: 3 Grams
Carbs: 7 Grams
Ingredients:

- 2 lbs. Parsnips, Peeled & Cut into Chunks
- 2 Tablespoons Maple Syrup
- 1 Tablespoon Olive Oil
- 1 Tablespoon Parsley Flakes

Directions:

1. Start by heating your air fryer to 360, and then add in your ingredients. Make sure that your parsnips are well coated.
2. Cook for forty minutes, and then serve warm.

Honey Roasted Carrots

Serves: 4
Time: 25 Minutes
Calories: 82
Protein: 1 Gram
Fat: 3.2 Grams
Carbs: 2.1 Grams
Ingredients:

- 1 Tablespoon Honey, Raw

- 3 Cups Baby Carrots

- 1 Tablespoon Olive Oil

- Sea Salt & Black Pepper to Taste

Directions:

1. Toss all of your ingredients into a bowl, and then heat your air fryer to 390. Cook for twelve minutes and serve warm.

Herb Vegetables

Serves: 4
Time: 30 Minutes
Calories: 41
Protein: 2 Grams
Fat: 1 Gram
Carbs: 5 Grams
Ingredients:

- 1 Red Bell Pepper, Sliced

- 8 Ounces Mushrooms, Sliced

- 1 Cup Green Beans, Chopped into 2 Inch Pieces

- 3 Cloves Garlic, Sliced

- 1/3 Cup Red Onion, Diced

- 1 Teaspoon Olive Oil

- ½ Teaspoon Basil

- ½ Teaspoon Tarragon

Directions:

1. Get out a bowl and mix together your red onion, red bell pepper, mushrooms, garlic and green beans. Drizzle your olive oil next, making sure everything is mixed and coasted. Add in your herbs, and toss again.

2. Place them in your air fryer basket, and roast until tender. This will take fourteen to eighteen minutes. Serve warm.

Crisp Broccoli

Serves: 4
Time: 25 Minutes
Calories: 63
Protein: 4 Grams
Fat: 2 Grams
Net Carbs: 10 Grams
Ingredients:

- 1 Tablespoon Lemon Juice, Fresh

- 2 Teaspoon Olive Oil

- 1 Head Broccoli

Directions:

1. Start by rinsing your broccoli and patting it dry. Cut it into florets, and then separate them. Make sure that if you use the stems it's cut into one inch chunks and peeled.

2. Toss your broccoli pieces with your lemon juice and olive oil until they're well coated. Roast your broccoli in batches for ten for fourteen minutes. Each. They should be tender and crisp, and then serve warm.

Roasted Bell Pepper

Serves: 4
Time: 30 Minutes
Calories: 36
Protein: 1 Gram
Fat: 1 Gram
Carbs: 5 Grams
Ingredients:

- 1 Teaspoon Olive Oil

- ½ Teaspoon Thyme

- 4 Cloves Garlic, Minced

- 4 Bell Peppers, Cut into Fourths

Directions:

1. Start by putting your peppers in your basket and drizzling with olive oil. Make sure they're coated well, and then roast for fifteen minutes.

2. Sprinkle with thyme and garlic, roasting for an additional three to five minutes. They should be tender, and serve warm.

Curried Brussels Sprouts

Serves: 4
Time: 30 Minutes
Calories: 86
Protein: 4 Grams
Fat: 3 Grams
Carbs: 12 Grams
Ingredients:

- 1 lb. Brussel Sprouts, end Trimmed & Halved
- 2 Teaspoons Olive Oil
- 1 Tablespoon Lemon Juice, Fresh
- 3 Teaspoons Curry Powder, Divided

Directions:

1. Start by getting gout a large bowl and mix together your olive oil with a teaspoon of curry powder. Toss your Brussel sprouts in, mixing until well coated. Place them in your air fryer basket, roasting for twelve minutes. During this cooking time you'll need to shake your basket once.

2. Sprinkle with the remaining curry powder and lemon juice, shaking your basket again. Roast for an additional three to five minutes. Your Brussel sprouts should be crisp and browned. Serve warm.

Garlic Asparagus

Serves: 4
Time: 15 Minutes
Calories: 41
protein: 3 Grams
Fat: 1 Gram
Carbs: 6 Grams
Ingredients:

- 1 lb. Asparagus, Rinsed & Trimmed
- 2 Teaspoons Olive Oil
- 3 Cloves Garlic, Minced
- 2 Tablespoons Balsamic Vinegar
- ½ Teaspoon Thyme

Directions:

1. Start by getting out a large bowl to toss your asparagus in olive oil before placing your vegetables in the basket.
2. Sprinkle with garlic before roasting for eight to eleven minutes. Your asparagus should be tender but crisp.
3. Drizzle with thyme and balsamic vinegar before serving warm.

Salmon Spring Rolls

Serves: 4
Time: 30 Minutes
Calories: 95
Protein: 13 Grams
Fat: 2 Grams
Carbs: 8 Grams
Ingredients:

- ½ lb. Salmon Fillet

- 1 Teaspoon Toasted Sesame Oil

- 1 Onion, Sliced

- * Rice Pepper Wrappers

- 1 Yellow Bell Pepper, Sliced Thin

- 1 Carrot, Shredded

- 1/3 Cup Flat Leaf Parsley, Fresh & Chopped

- ¼ Cup Basil, Fresh & Chopped

Directions:

1. Start by placing your salmon in the air fryer, drizzling it with sesame oil and add in your onion. Cook for eight to ten minutes. Your onion should be tender and the salmon should flake easily.

2. While this is cooking get out a shallow bowl and fill it with warm water.

3. Dip your rice paper wrappers in one at a time. Make sure to place them on a clean work surface.

4. Top each wrapper with a bit of the salmon and onion mixture, bell pepper, carrot, basil and parsley. Roll the wrappers up making sure to close them.

5. Air fry at 380 for seven to eight minutes. Cut in half before serving warm.

Baby Potatoes

Serves: 2
Time: 15 Minutes
Calories: 94
Protein: 3.3 Grams
Fat: 2.5 Grams
Carbs: 15.9 Grams
Ingredients:

- 250 Grams Baby Potatoes, Halved
- 1 Teaspoon Olive Oil
- ¼ Teaspoon Oregano Powder
- 1/8 Teaspoon Garlic Powder
- 1/8 Teaspoon Thyme
- 1/8 Teaspoon Sea Salt, Fine
- 1/8 Teaspoon Black Pepper

Directions:

1. Start by heating your air fryer to 350, and then wash and half your baby potatoes.

2. Toss these halves in olive oil, garlic powder, oregano, salt, pepper and thyme. Place them on a baking sheet accessory, roasting in your air fryer for thirty minutes. You'll need to shake in about five minutes to make sure that all parts are exposed and will become crisp. Serve warm.

Roasted Curry Vegetables

Serves: 4
Time: 30 Minutes
Calories: 165
Protein: 2.5 Grams
Fat: 7.4 Grams
Carbs: 24.3 Grams
Ingredients:

- 2 Cups Sweet Potatoes, Cubed
- 1 Zucchini, Large & Diced with Skin On
- 2 Tablespoons Olive Oil
- 1 Cup Mushrooms
- ½ Teaspoon Curry Powder
- 1/8 Teaspoon Sea Salt
- 1/8 Teaspoon Black Pepper
- ½ Cup Water
- ½ Teaspoon Turmeric Powder
- 1 Tablespoon Alfalfa Sprouts

Directions:

1. Start by heating your air fryer to 375.

2. Get out a baking dish and add in your button mushrooms, sweet potatoes, zucchini, olive oil, turmeric, salt, water, pepper and curry powder in. mix until well combined.

3. Place it in your air fryer to cook for a half hour, and make sure to mix it every ten minutes. Add additional water as needed so that your vegetables don't dry out.

4. Serve warm and topped with alfalfa sprouts.

Desperts

Strawberry Cheesecake Rolls

Serves: 12
Time: 20 Minutes
Calories: 98
Protein: 3 Grams
Fat: 5 Grams
Carbs: 12 Grams
Ingredients:

- 1/3 Cup Strawberries, Sliced Fresh
- 1 Tablespoon Strawberry Preserves
- 4 Ounces Cream Cheese
- 8 Ounce Can Crescent Rolls
- Cooking Oil

Directions:

1. Start by rolling out your dough int o a large rectangle, cutting twelve rectangles from it. You'll need to make two cuts lengthwise and three cuts crosswise.

2. Put your cream cheese in a microwave safe bowl, and then microwave for fifteen minutes so that it softens.

3. In a medium bowl combine your strawberry preserves and cream cheese, mixing well.

4. Scoop two teaspoons of this mixture onto each piece, and spread it out. Just make sure you don't go to the edges of the dough. Add fresh strawberries to each.

5. Roll each rectangle up to create a roll, and then spray your air fryer basket down with cooking oil.

6. Put your rolls in the basket, but do not stack them. If you do, they'll cook together, so it's better to cook them in batches. Cook for eight minutes, and allow them to cool for two to three minutes before removing them from your air fryer basket. Repeat until all of your remaining rolls are cooked, and allow them to cool before serving.

Mini Chocolate Cake

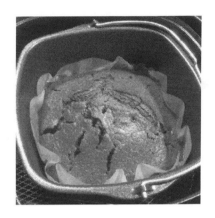

Serves: 2
Time: 20 Minutes
Calories: 403
Protein: 4 Grams
Fat: 30 Grams
Carbs: 6.9 Grams
Ingredients:

- 2 Tablespoons Cocoa Powder
- ¼ Cup Sugar
- ¼ Cup Flour
- 1/8 Teaspoon Sea Salt, Fine
- 1/8 Teaspoon Baking Soda
- 3 Tablespoons Whole Milk
- 2 Tablespoon Olive Oil
- 1 Tablespoon Water
- ¼ Teaspoon Vanilla Extract, Pure

Directions:

1. Get outa bowl and combine your cocoa powder, baking soda, sugar, salt, and flour. Stir until well combined.

2. Get out a separate bowl and combine your vanilla, oil, water and milk. Stir well.

3. Stir all of your dry and wet ingredients together until it forms a smooth batter, and then grease two ramekins. Divide between the dishes, and preheat your air fryer to 325. Cover the bottom with parchment paper, and place the ramekins in. cook for five minutes, and allow to cool before serving.

Blueberry Scones

Serves: 10

Time: 20 Minutes

Calories: 130

Protein: 3 Grams

Fat: 2 Grams

Carbs: 4 Grams

Ingredients:

- 2 Teaspoon Vanilla Extract, Pure
- 2 Teaspoon Baking Powder
- 5 Tablespoons Sugar
- ½ Cup Butter
- ½ Cup Heavy Cream
- 2 Eggs
- 1 Cup White Flour
- 1 Cup Blueberries

Directions:

1. Start by mixing your baking soda, salt, flour, and blueberries. Stir well.

2. Get out a bowl and mix your heavy cream, vanilla extract, butter, eggs and sugar. Stir well, and then combine both measures together to form a dough. Shape ten triangles from this mixture, and then preheat your air fryer to 320. Cook for ten minutes, and serve chilled.

Easy Macaroons

Serves: 20

Time: 20 Minutes

Calories: 55

Protein: 1 Gram

Fat: 6 Grams

Carbs: 2 Grams

Ingredients:

- 2 Tablespoons Sugar
- 1 Teaspoon Vanilla Extract, Pure
- 2 Cups Coconut, Shredded
- 4 Egg Whites

Directions:

1. Get out a bowl and mix your sugar and egg whites together using a mixer, and then add in your vanilla extract and coconut. Shape into small balls, and then cook for eight minutes in your air fryer at 340 degrees.
2. Allow to cool before serving.

Black Tea Cake

Serves: 12
Time: 45 Minutes
Calories: 200
Protein: 2 Grams
Fat: 4 Grams
Carbs: 6 Grams
Ingredients:

- 4 Eggs

- 2 Cups Sugar

- ½ Cup Butter

- 6 Tablespoons Black Tea Powder

- 2 Cups Whole Milk

- ½ Cup Olive Oil

- 2 Teaspoons Vanilla Extract, Pure

- 3 ½ Cups Flour

- 1 Teaspoon Baking Soda

- 3 Teaspoons Baking Powder

Cream:

- 6 Tablespoons Honey
- 1 Cup Butter, Softened
- 4 Cups Sugar

Directions:

1. Start by putting your milk in a pot, heating it over medium heat. Add in your tea and stir well. Take it off heat, allowing it to cool down.
2. Get out a bowl and mix a half a cup of butter with two cups of sugar, vegetable oil, eggs, vanilla extract, baking soda, baking powder, and your flour. Mix well.
3. Proud this mixture into two round pans that have been greased.
4. Cook in your air fryer at 330 for twenty-five minutes.
5. In a bowl mix your honey, four cups of sugar and a cup of butter. Stir until it's well combined.
6. Spread your cream all over the top of the cake once its cooled, and cool it down before serving.

Plum Cake

Serves: 8
Time: 2 Hours 5 Minutes
Calories: 192
Protein: 7 Grams
Fat: 4 Grams
Carbs: 6 Grams
Ingredients:

- 1 Ounce Butter, Softened

- 1 Package Dried yeast

- 7 Ounces Flour

- 1 Egg, Whisked

- 5 Tablespoons Sugar

- 1 ¾ lbs. Plumps, Pitted & Quartered

- 3 Ounces Whole Milk, Warm

- 1 Lemon, Zested

- 1 Ounce Almond Flakes

Directions:

1. Start by getting out a bowl and mix your flour, three tablespoons of sugar, yeast and butter. Mix well before adding in your egg and milk, whisking for four minutes so a dough forms.
2. Get out a spring form pan and arrange your dough in it. Make sure you grease your pan with butter first, and then set it to the side for an hour.
3. Arrange your plumps on top of the butter, sprinkling the rest of your sugar on it.
4. Cook at 350 in your air fryer for thirty-six minutes, and sprinkle with lemon zest and almond flakes before serving.

Lentil Cookies

Serves: 36
Time: 35 Minutes
Calories: 154
Protein: 7 Grams
Fat: 2 Grams
Carbs: 4 Grams
Ingredients:

- 1 Cup Water

- 1 Cup Whole Wheat Flour

- 1 Cup Lentils, Canned, Drained & Mashed

- 1 Cup White Flour

- 1 Teaspoon Cinnamon Powder

- 1 Teaspoon Baking Powder

- 1 Cup Butter, Softened

- ½ Teaspoon Nutmeg, Ground

- ½ Cup Brown Sugar

- 1 Cup Rolled Oats

- ½ Cup White Sugar

- 1 Egg

- 2 teaspoons Almond Extract

- 1 Cup Raisins

- 1 Cup Coconut, Unsweetened & Shredded

Directions:

1. Get out a bowl and mix your white and whole wheat flour with your baking powder, salt, cinnamon and nutmeg. Stir until well combined.

2. In another bowl mix your white sugar, brown sugar and butter, mixing for two minutes using a kitchen mixer.

3. Add in your lentils, almond extract, egg, flour mix, oats, raisins, and coconut. Stir until everything is well combined.

4. Scoop tablespoons of dough onto a baking sheet that will fit in your air fryer. You'll need to cook in batches.

5. Cook at 350 for fifteen minutes, and serve once cooled.

Date & Lentil Brownies

Serves: 8
Time: 25 Minutes
Calories: 162
Protein: 4 Grams
Fat: 4 Grams
Carbs: 3 Grams
Ingredients:

- 28 Ounces Lentils, Canned, Rinsed & Drained

- 12 Dates

- 1 Tablespoon Honey, Raw

- 1 Banana, Peeled & Chopped

- ½ Teaspoon Baking Soda

- 4 Tablespoons Almond Butter

- 2 Tablespoons Cocoa Powder

Directions:

1. Start by mixing your butter, banana, cocoa, baking soda, honey and lentils in a food processor. Blend well before adding in your dates and pulsing a

few more times. Pour this into a greased pan that will fit into your air fryer. Make sure that it's spread evenly, and then cook at 360 for fifteen minutes.

2. Allow them to cool before slicing to serve.

Dark Chocolate & Oatmeal Cookies

Serves: 30
Time: 25 Minutes
Calories: 55
Protein: 1 Gram
Fat: 2 Grams
Carbs: 8 Grams
Ingredients:

- 3 Tablespoons Butter, Unsalted

- 1 Cup Oatmeal, Quick Cooking

- 2 Ounces Dark Chocolate, Chopped

- 2 Egg Whites

- ½ Cup Brown Sugar, Packed

- 1 Teaspoon Vanilla Extract, Pure

- ½ Cup Pastry Flour, Whole Wheat

- ¼ Cup Cranberries, Dried

- ½ Teaspoon Baking Soda

Directions:

1. Start by getting out a metal medium owl and mix together your dark chocolate and butter. Bake for one to three minutes in your air fryer. Your chocolate should melt, and then stir the mixture smooth.

2. Add in your brown sugar, vanilla and egg whites, beating until smooth.

3. Add in your oatmeal, baking soda and pastry flour. Stir in your cranberries, and make a dough.

4. Form thirty one inch balls, and cook in batches of eight in your air fryer for seven to ten minutes.

5. Allow them to cool before serving.

Maple Cupcakes

Serves: 4
Time: 30 Minutes
Calories: 150
Protein: 4 Grams
Fat: 3 Grams
Carbs: 5 Grams
Ingredients:

- 4 Teaspoons Maple Syrup
- ½ Apple, Cored & Chopped
- ¾ Cup White Flour
- ½ Teaspoon Baking Powder
- 1 Teaspoon Vanilla Extract, Pure
- 4 Tablespoons Butter
- ½ Cup Applesauce
- 4 Eggs
- 2 Teaspoons Cinnamon, Ground

Directions:

1. Start by heating up a pan with butter, placing it over medium heat. Add in your maple syrup, applesauce, vanilla and eggs. Stir well and then take off heat. Allow the mixture to cool down, and then add in your baking powder, apples, cinnamon and flour. Whisk well, and then pour into a cupcake pan that fits in your air fryer. You may have to do this n batches.

2. Heat your air fryer to 350, and cook for twenty minutes. Allow your cupcakes to cool before serving.

Mandarin Pudding

Serves: 8
Time: 1 Hour
Calories: 162
Protein: 6 Grams
Fat: 3 Grams
Carbs: 3 Grams
Ingredients:

- 2 Eggs, Whisked

- 4 Ounces Butter, Softened

- 2 Tablespoons Brown Sugar

- 2 Mandarins, Juiced

- 1 Mandarin, Peeled & Sliced

- ¾ Cup Sugar

- ¾ Cup Almonds, Ground

- ¾ Cup White Flour

- Honey for Serving

Directions:

1. Get out a loaf pan that fits in your air fryer, and grease it with butter. Sprinkle brown sugar at the bottom before arranging your mandarin slices on top.

2. get out a bowl and mix your eggs, almonds, flour, butter and mandarin juices together. Stir well, and then spoon this over the mandarin slices.

3. Cook at 360 for forty minutes, and then drizzle with honey before serving.

Ricotta Lemon Cake

Serves: 4
Time: 1 Hour 20 Minutes
Calories: 110
Protein: 4 Grams
Fat: 3 Grams
Carbs: 3 Grams
Ingredients:

- 8 Eggs, Whisked

- 1/2 lb. Sugar

- 3 lbs. Ricotta Cheese

- 1 Lemon, Zested

- 1 Orange, Zested

- Butter for Greasing

Directions:

1. Start by getting out a bowl and mix your sugar, cheese, eggs, orange zest and lemon zest together. Stir well, and then grease a baking pan that fits in your air fryer. Spread the batter in it, and then cook at 390 for thirty minutes. Reduce your heat to 380, and cook for an additional forty minutes.

2. Allow to cool down before serving.

Tangerine Cake

Serves: 8
Time: 30 Minutes
Calories: 190
Protein: 4 Grams
Fat: 1 Gram
Carbs: 4 Grams
Ingredients:

- ½ Teaspoon Vanilla Extract, Pure

- 2 Lemons, Juiced & Zested

- 1 Tangerine, Juiced & Zested

- Tangerine Segments for Serving

- ¾ Cup White Sugar

- 2 Cups Flour

- ¼ Cup Olive Oil

- ½ Cup Whole Milk

- 1 Teaspoon Apple Cider Vinegar

Directions:

1. Start by mixing your flour and sugar in a bowl. Stir well, and then get out another bowl to mix your oil, vinegar, vanilla extract, milk, lemon zest, lemon juice, and tangerine zest, and tangerine juice. Whisk well.

2. Add your flour in, and then pour it into your cake pan. Make sure the cake pan fits in your air fryer, and cook at 360 for twenty minutes.

3. Serve topped with tangerine segments.

Grilled Cinnamon Pineapple

Serves: 2
Time: 20 Minutes
Calories: 276
Protein: 4.6 Grams
Fat: 5.3 Grams
Carbs: 4.2 Grams
Ingredients:

- 4 Pineapple Slices

- 2 Tablespoons Sugar

- 1 Teaspoon Cinnamon

Directions:

1. Start by adding your sugar and cinnamon into a zipper top bag, and shake well. Add in your pineapple slices, shaking until they're well coated. Allow it to marinate in the fridge for twenty minutes, and then preheat your air fryer for five minutes.

2. Place your pineapple pieces in the air fryer once it's heated to 360, and then grill for ten minutes. Flip and grill for an additional ten minutes.

Blueberry Pudding

Serves: 6
Time: 35 Minutes
Calories: 150
Protein: 4 Grams
Fat: 3 Grams
Carbs: 7 Grams
Ingredients:

- 3 Tablespoons Maple syrup
- 2 Tablespoons Rosemary, Fresh & Chopped
- 2 Cups Flour
- 2 Cups Rolled Oats
- 8 Cups Blueberries, fresh
- 1 Stick Butter, Melted
- 1 Cup Walnuts, Chopped

Directions:

1. Start by spreading your blueberries in a greased pan that fits in your air fryer.

2. Get out a food processor and mix your flour, walnuts, butter, oats, maple syrup and rosemary. Blend well, and then place this over your blueberries.

3. Cook at 350 for twenty-five minutes. Allow it to cool before slicing to serve.

Berry Mix

Serves: 4

Time: 12 Minutes

Calories: 163

Protein: 2.1 Grams

Fat: 4 Grams

Carbs: 10 Grams

Ingredients:

- 2 Tablespoons Lemon Juice, Fresh
- 1 ½ Tablespoons Champagne Vinegar
- 1 ½ Tablespoons Maple Syrup
- 1 lb. Strawberries, Halved
- 1 Tablespoon Olive Oil
- 1 ½ Cups Blueberries, Fresh
- ¼ Cup Basil Leaves, Fresh & Torn

Directions:

1. Start by getting out a pan that fits into your air fryer, and mix all ingredients together until well combined.
2. Heat your air fryer to 310, and cook for six minutes.
3. Sprinkle with basil before serving either warm or chilled.

Conclusion

Now you know everything you need to in order to get started with your air fryer! Just pick a recipe to get started with low sodium, low carb cooking in no time at all. Remember that healthy food doesn't mean that you need to slave away in the kitchen or pay big bucks for hand delivered meals. All you need is to try new, delicious recipes that are sure to become family favorites in no time at all. Your air fryer will soon be the most used item in your kitchen!

Made in the USA
Middletown, DE
10 August 2019